*T*his book presented to

Chris Bard

by

Lance Long

12-25-03
date

May God enrich your life,
your love and your relationships.

Merry Christmas

Resources by Les and Leslie Parrott

Books

Becoming Soul Mates
Getting Ready for the Wedding
Love Is
The Love List
The Marriage Mentor Manual
Meditations on Proverbs for Couples
Questions Couples Ask
Relationships
Relationships Workbook
Saving Your Marriage Before It Starts
Saving Your Marriage Before It Starts Workbook for Men
Saving Your Marriage Before It Starts Workbook for Women
Saving Your Second Marriage Before It Starts
Saving Your Second Marriage Before It Starts Workbook for Men
Saving Your Second Marriage Before It Starts Workbook for Women
When Bad Things Happen to Good Marriages

Video Curriculum — Zondervan Groupware™

Relationships
Saving Your Marriage Before It Starts
Mentoring Engaged and Newlywed Couples

Audio Pages®

Relationships
Saving Your Marriage Before It Starts
Saving Your Second Marriage Before It Starts
When Bad Things Happen to Good Marriages

Books by Les Parrott III

High-Maintenance Relationships
Life You Want Your Kids to Live
Seven Secrets of a Healthy Dating Relationship
Once Upon a Family

Books by Leslie Parrott

If You Ever Needed Friends, It's Now
God Loves You Nose to Toes (children's book)

$\mathcal{L}$ove
is...

Meditations for Couples

on 1 Corinthians 13

Les & Leslie Parrott

GRAND RAPIDS, MICHIGAN 49530 USA

ZONDERVAN™

Love Is
Copyright © 1999 by Les and Leslie Parrott

Requests for information should be addressed to:

Zondervan, *Grand Rapids, Michigan 49530*

Library of Congress Cataloging-in-Publication Data

Parrott, Les.
    Love is : meditations for couples on I Corinthians 13 / Les and Leslie
  Parrott.
       p.   cm.
    ISBN: 0-310-21666-4
    1. Bible. N.T. Corinthians, 1st, XIII—Meditations.   2. Love—Religious
  aspects—Christianity—Meditations.   3. Spouses—Religious life.
  I. Parrott, Leslie L.,   1964–   . II. Title.
  BS2675.6.L6P37   1998
  242'.644—dc21   98-44037
                                                CIP

Translations quoted include: *Basic Bible Translation* copyright © 1950 by E. P.
Dutton & Co., Inc.; *Berkeley Version* copyright © 1958 by Zondervan
Publishing House; *Cotton Patch Version of Paul's Epistles* copyright © 1968 by
Clarence Jordan; *Letters to Young Churches* by J. B. Phillips copyright © 1947
by The Macmillan Company; *The King James Version; The Letters to the
Corinthians* by William Barclay; *The Living Bible* copyright © 1971 by Tyndale
House Publishers; *The Message* copyright © 1993 by Eugene H. Peterson; *New
American Bible* copyright © 1970 by Confraternity of Christian Doctrine; *New
International Readers' Version* copyright © 1994, 1996 by International Bible
Society; *New International Version* copyright © 1973, 1978, 1984 by
International Bible Society; *Ronald Knox* copyright © 1944 by Sheed & Ward,
Inc.; *Twentieth Century New Testament* copyright © 1900 by Fleming H. Revell
Company; *Wuest's Expanded Translation of the Greek New Testament* © 1958
by Wm. B. Eerdmans Publishing Company. In addition, every effort was made
to contact Angela McCord for her permission and to locate publishing
information for J. Oswald Sanders.

This edition printed on acid-free paper.

Interior design by Sherri L. Hoffman

Printed in the United States of America

---

03 04 05 06 07 08 /❖ DC/ 13 12 11 10 9 8 7 6

To J. Paul and Marilyn Turner,
a couple whose commitment
to married love
is matched by their
selfless service to others

Contents

The Most Excellent Way

What is the *summum bonum* — the supreme good?"
With this question Professor Henry Drummond
began his famous lecture "The Greatest Thing in the
World." The year was 1883 as he stood before a class-
room of college students and drove home the question:
"You have life before you. Once only can you live it.
What is the noblest object of desire, the supreme gift to
covet?"

The rhetorical question required no reply. Everyone
knew the answer. Love. Love is the ultimate good. It lifts
us outside ourselves. Love sees beyond the normal range
of human vision — over walls of resentment and barriers
of betrayal. Love rises above the petty demands and con-
flicts of life and inspires our spirit to transcend who we
are tempted to settle for: decent, but merely mediocre.
Love aims higher. Unencumbered by self-absorption,
love charms us to reach our ideal. Love allures us with a

If there is anything better than to be loved it is loving. *Anonymous*

hint of what might be possible. No question about it. Love is the *summum bonum* — "the most excellent way."

And no words, no passage, no song or poem in all of human history has crystallized the qualities of love into simple absolutes more elegantly than 1 Corinthians 13. The Love Chapter of the Bible paints a perfect picture of love. It reveals the ideal love everyone yearns for. But something about these words, the way they are written, tells us they are meant to be not only admired but also lived. These words are a means to a more excellent way of being.

While the passage draws a profile of ideal love, it is too plainly spoken to be a mere mystical flight of fancy. Paul, the writer of these words, was surely inspired as he penned these words. But the passage is not a fantasy of what might be nice. It is a serious essay on how love can be lived. Love is patient. It is not jealous, does not get angry quickly. These are qualities ordinary people can cultivate to build extraordinary relationships. The challenge, of course, is to find ways of bringing these heavenly qualities into our earthly reality.

On the ground floor of our home is a study lined with wraparound bookshelves. And one of these shelves holds forty or fifty Bibles. We've collected them over the years. Some were given to us to mark a meaningful milestone; others were bought for teaching and study. They come in all sizes and colors — the King James, the New

Life has taught us that love does not consist in gazing at each other but in looking outward together in the same direction.
Antoine de Saint-Exupery

King James, the Good News, the New American Standard, the Amplified, the New International Version, and on and on. When a new version of the Bible is published, chances are we will obtain a copy. And when we do, one of the first places we'll turn is 1 Corinthians 13. These verses seem like a good starting point for breaking in a new Bible. And over the years, we've noticed that reading these words in different versions allows the heavenly qualities of perfect love to more easily take root in our earthly lives.

There is no single version of the Scriptures for everyone. One size and color does not fit and serve all. While God's message is singular, unified, and unchanging, its translations take many forms. And when it comes to taking hold of love's ideal in our own life, the heart and mind come closer to living love's message when we read it from different pens. Consider the stark contrast of Elizabethan English from the King James Version compared to Eugene Peterson's contemporary translation from *The Message*:

> Though I speak with the tongues of men and of angels, and have not charity, I am become as sounding brass, or a tinkling cymbal.

> If I speak with human eloquence and angelic ecstasy but don't love, I'm nothing but the creaking of a rusty gate.

*A*t the touch of love everyone becomes a poet. *Plato*

While the message is undoubtedly the same in each translation, the tone and turn of each phrase reveals a different path toward understanding and living out the ideals of the most excellent way. For the chapter titles, however, we chose to use the most popular English translation of the Bible, the New International Version.

Our friend and former professor Lewis Smedes has said, "Ideal love does not work in an ideal world. It works within the limits of our ordinary lives." As you read the different translations of Paul's love passage contained in this book, we pray that each line will show you the power of selfless love to change our self-interested lives. And we pray that each reading will draw you closer to God, the author of love. For it is only in relationship with God that we come close to living love's ideal.

Les and Leslie Parrott
Center for Relationship Development
Seattle Pacific University

It is love, not reason, that is stronger than death.   *Thomas Mann*

If I Speak

If I speak in the tongues of men and of angels,
but have not love, I am only a resounding gong or a
clanging cymbal. —*New International Version*

We couldn't count how many times we have stood before a group of couples and talked about talking. In nearly every conceivable corner of North America and in several places around the world, we have demonstrated techniques and tools for improving a couples' communication. And it would be impossible to add up the number of times a couple has come into our counseling office after a communication meltdown in their marriage. "We just don't communicate" is the common refrain. What's more, it would be embarrassing to see the tallies on the number of times we have personally failed in our marriage to follow our own advice when it comes to "talking our talk." Yet we — and nearly

---

Take away love and our earth is a tomb.   *Robert Browning*

every couple we have the privilege of working with — keep trying.

Why? Because communication is the lifeblood of marriage. More than any other skill, the competence to say what we mean and understand what we hear is paramount to building a lasting relationship. Without effective communication we lose the ability to understand and be understood. Without communication we lose at love.

No wonder Paul begins his litany of love by saying: "If I speak ... but have not love, I am only a resounding gong or a clanging cymbal." In other words, it doesn't matter how well-spoken and eloquent you are. You may have mastered the technique of "reflecting your partner's feelings" before making your own point. You may be great at using "I" statements (rather than the accusatory "you" statements) in your conversation. You may be naturally gifted as a powerfully persuasive and charismatic communicator. You may speak like an angel, but if you don't walk your talk, if you don't have love in your heart, you might as well bang pots and pans together. Because that's how annoying you will become.

As a psychologist (Les) and a marriage and family therapist (Leslie), we can tell you that almost every communication problem in marriage can be traced to a lack of love. Not that the couple isn't "in love." It's just that they aren't working to be more loving, less selfish. Think

The biggest disease today is not leprosy or tuberculosis, but rather the feeling of being unwanted, uncared for, and deserted by everybody. The greatest evil is the lack of love. *Mother Teresa*

about it. Whenever you set aside self-seeking ways, communication problems fade. Of course, couples don't often want to hear this. They are interested in new verbal strategies, more techniques and tools. And in most counseling offices that's exactly what they get. But ultimately tools by themselves don't work. Why? Because you can practice all the communication techniques in the world and still end up sounding like nothing more than an annoying clang.

On a few occasions we have tried to write our own interpretation of Paul's love poem. Here's the first sentence of one of our versions: "If I go to marriage seminars and read marriage books to learn new verbal strategies, and I never set aside my own self-centered desires, I'm nothing more than an annoying tape recorder that replays my partner's messages."

Communication skills are important to learn — no doubt about it — but they fall flat without love. They turn into tools of manipulation. "You're just doing that thing our counselor said to do" is the response a new technique often elicits in the absence of love.

So before you try to tune up your talk, overhaul your heart. Allow love to seize every word, every syllable. Invite love to lay claim to your conversation. Forgo the annoyance of clanging cymbals and enjoy the full rhapsody of your love song.

*L*et your conversation be always full of grace. *Colossians 4:6*

1 Corinthians 13

New International Version

*A*nd now I will show you the most excellent way.

If I speak in the tongues of men and of angels, but have not love, I am only a resounding gong or a clanging cymbal. If I have the gift of prophecy and can fathom all mysteries and all knowledge, and if I have a faith that can move mountains, but have not love, I am nothing. If I give all I possess to the poor and surrender my body to the flames, but have not love, I gain nothing.

Love is patient, love is kind. It does not envy, it does not boast, it is not proud. It is not rude, it is not self-seeking, it is not easily angered, it keeps no record of wrongs. Love does not delight in evil but rejoices with the truth. It always protects, always trusts, always hopes, always perseveres.

Love never fails. But where there are prophecies, they will cease; where there are tongues, they will be stilled; where there is knowledge, it will pass away. For we know in part and we prophesy in part, but when perfection comes, the imperfect disappears. When I was a child, I talked like a child, I thought like a child, I reasoned like a child. When I became a man, I put childish ways behind me. Now we see but a poor reflection as in a mirror; then we shall see face to face. Now I know in part; then I shall know fully, even as I am fully known.

And now these three remain: faith, hope and love. But the greatest of these is love.

Love Is Patient

Charity suffereth long. — *King James Version*

*F*rom one of the great dynasties in China comes an apocryphal story of a wise man who had the most extraordinary relationships. He got along with everyone. He never argued with friends or family members. His children were kind and polite. He enjoyed remarkable harmony inside and outside of his home.

News of this insightful man traveled to the Chinese emperor, who was so impressed that he ordered the man to write a great scroll describing how others could produce such outstanding relationships with friends and family. The emperor declared by royal proclamation that the scroll was to contain ten thousand words.

The man was sent off to write. Days later he delivered a heavy scroll to the emperor's palace. The scroll was immediately taken to the great hall where it was rolled out across a huge table. The emperor began to read as observers stood silent. After a few minutes, the

*O*ur patience will achieve more than our force.   *Edmund Burke*

emperor slowly nodded his approval, and the onlookers breathed a sigh of relief.

As requested, the man had written ten thousand words — but it was the same word written again and again: *Patience. Patience. Patience.*

Every loving heart overflows with patience. Perhaps this is why Paul begins his litany of loving qualities with this one in particular. Patience, that ability to calmly endure difficulty or inconvenience without complaint, is the love a mother shows a tiresome toddler. Patience is the love a husband gives a wife who's running late. And patience is the love a teacher shows a student learning to read and write.

If you boil patience down to its essence, it is the loving response to frustration. Think about it. Frustration tests our threshold for patience. If you have ever watched a small child trying to thread a needle, your patience has been tested. You see the child, again and again, trying to push the blunt and frazzled end of the thread through the eye of an unsteady needle. Do you wait two trials, four trials, six trials before snatching it away and doing it yourself? How much frustration can you tolerate before intervening? How long can you suffer? Long enough to take a quiet breath and to let her eventually ask for help?

It's not surprising that this translation says "charity suffereth long." Patience is measured by our ability to endure something we'd rather not. Each of us is destined

*P*atience is a bitter plant but it bears sweet fruit.   *German proverb*

to suffer. But not as passive victims. Love suffers long not because its strength is in endurance but because its power is in the future. Patience empowers love to work on a troubled marriage. Patience empowers love to care for a troubled child. Patience empowers love to accept our troubled selves.

Love is patient. And just as our patience is almost exhausted, love empowers us to find a little more.

They also serve who only stand and wait. *John Milton*

1 Corinthians 13

King James Version

*Y*et shew I unto you a more excellent way.

Though I speak with the tongues of men and of angels, and have not charity, I am become as sounding brass, or a tinkling cymbal.

And though I have the gift of prophecy, and understand all mysteries, and all knowledge; and though I have all faith, so that I could remove mountains, and have not charity, I am nothing.

And though I bestow all my goods to feed the poor, and though I give my body to be burned, and have not charity, it profiteth me nothing.

Charity suffereth long, and is kind; charity envieth not; charity vaunteth not itself, is not puffed up,

Doth not behave itself unseemly, seeketh not her own, is not easily provoked, thinketh no evil;

Rejoiceth not in iniquity, but rejoiceth in the truth;

Beareth all things, believeth all things, hopeth all things, endureth all things.

Charity never faileth: but whether there be prophecies, they shall fail; whether there be tongues, they shall cease; whether there be knowledge, it shall vanish away.

For we know in part, and we prophesy in part.

But when that which is perfect is come, then that which is in part shall be done away.

When I was a child, I spake as a child, I understood as a child, I thought as a child: but when I became a man, I put away childish things.

For now we see through a glass, darkly; but then face to face: now I know in part; but then shall I know even as also I am known.

And now abideth faith, hope, charity, these three; but the greatest of these is charity.

Love Is Kind

> Love is kind, gentle, benign, pervading and
> penetrating the whole nature, mellowing all
> which would have been harsh and austere.
> — *Wuest's Expanded Translation*

*Y*ou didn't need to do that."

"I know — I wanted to," Les replied.

All morning I was working like mad to complete a report due after lunch. It was an unusually hot, muggy, Seattle morning in August, and I was parked at the kitchen table in front of my laptop computer when Les quietly slipped in and set up a fan to cool the room.

"I don't know if it will make any difference," Les said, trying to place the fan in just the right place, "but I thought it was worth a try."

I don't know if the fan did anything to alleviate the oppressive heat that morning, but I do recall feeling suddenly soothed by my husband's kindness. Why? Because he didn't have to go to the trouble of scrounging around

---

our basement, still wearing his pre-shower bathrobe, to find our old fan in an attempt to make me feel better. I didn't ask him to do it. He never even heard me complain about the heat. He wasn't looking for appreciation, to make amends, or to get something in return. No, this was sheer kindness.

It's easy to gloss over the simple idea that "love is kind" while reading Paul's Love Chapter. But if we do skip over this critical quality of love, we are missing out on one of the most revolutionary relationship truths in the universe. Kindness is an integral part of love because it stems from an uncalculating attitude that desires neither monetary payment nor human applause.

A favorite definition: *Kindness is love's readiness to enhance the life of another person.* Is there anything more loving than kindness? Is there anything more thoughtful, more empathic, more sweet, than improving another person's situation only for the joy of seeing it enriched?

Kindness comes from small behaviors. We don't think of big donations or grand contributions as "kind." We call them "generous," "charitable," or "benevolent," but it is the small things we call "kind." Kindness, for example, comes when we turn down our partner's side of the bed before crawling into it ourselves. Kindness comes when we readjust the car seat after driving so our partner doesn't

If you stop to be kind, you must swerve often from your path.
Mary Webb

have to. Kindness comes when we load the dishwasher when it's not our turn. Kindness comes from a million small behaviors that enhance the life of the one we love. That's why Kenneth Wuest's translation of Paul's love poem underscores the gentle kindness of love as "mellowing all which would have been harsh and austere."

Kindness sets aside the fear that we will be exploited. It relinquishes self-focus and is energized by the needs of another. Kindness causes us to pause from our own pursuits in order to augment somebody else's life. Make no mistake about it: Once we remove kindness from a loving heart it is only a matter of time before the heart atrophies and love is lost altogether.

It is futile to judge a kind deed by its motives. Kindness can become its own motive. We are made kind by being kind. Eric Hoffer

1 Corinthians 13

Wuest's Expanded Translation

*A*nd yet I point out a superexcellent way.

If in the languages of men I speak and the languages of the angels but do not have love [Greek word here used of God's love produced in the heart of the yielded saint by the Holy Spirit, a love that impels one to deny himself for the sake of the loved one], I have already become and at present am sounding brass or a clanging cymbal. And if I have the gift of uttering divine revelations and know all the mysteries and all the knowledge, and if I have all the faith so that I am able to keep on removing mountain after mountain, but am not possessing love, I am nothing. And if I use all my possessions to feed the poor, and if I deliver up my body [as a martyr] in order that I may glory, but do not have love, I am being profited in not even one thing.

Love meekly and patiently bears ill treatment from others. Love is kind, gentle, benign, pervading and penetrating the whole nature, mellowing all which would have been harsh and austere; is not envious. Love does not brag, nor does it show itself off, is not ostentatious, does not have an inflated ego, does not act unbecomingly, does not seek after the things which are its own, is not irritated, provoked, exasperated, aroused to anger, does not take into account the evil [which it suffers], does not rejoice at the iniquity but rejoices with the truth, endures all things, believes all things, hopes all things, bears up under all things, not losing heart nor courage. Love never fails.

But whether there are utterances given by a person consisting of divine revelations he has received, they shall cease; whether languages, they shall stop, whether knowledge, it shall be done away; for we know in a partial, fragmentary, incomplete way, and we utter divine revelations in the same way. But whenever that which is complete comes, that which is incomplete and fragmentary will be done away. When I was a child I was accustomed to speak as a child. I used to understand as a child. I was accustomed to reason as a child. When I have become a man and have the status of an adult, I have permanently put away the things of a child, for we are seeing now by means of a mirror obscurely, but then, face to face. Now I know only in a fragmentary fashion, but then I shall fully know even as also I was known. But now there remains faith, hope, love; these three. But the greatest of these is this previously mentioned love.

Love Does Not Envy

Love doesn't want what it doesn't have.
— *The Message*

*T*he devil was crossing the Libyan desert when he came upon a few of his friends who were tormenting a holy man. This man, however, easily shook off their evil suggestions. As the devil watched these imps unsuccessfully try to drag this man down, he stepped forward to give them a little advice.

"Permit me to show you how it is done," the devil said. With that he whispered to the holy man: "Your brother has just been made Bishop of Alexandria." A scowl of envy at once clouded the serene face of the man, and his whole demeanor drooped. "That," said the devil to his imps, "is what I recommend."

And for good reason. Envy will sabotage even the most devoted person's ability to love. Sometimes it starts out as jealousy. Every person of every age knows what it

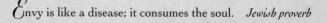

*E*nvy is like a disease; it consumes the soul.   *Jewish proverb*

is like to be jealous of friends and family members. Say, for example, your friend shows up at work in an attractive new outfit, and you toss out an honest compliment: "Nice suit. I'm jealous." You'd like a new outfit too. Who wouldn't? And unless there is something more to your message, you have little to worry about. But if you're secretly hoping your coworker's clothes get stained over lunch, look out! That's when gentle jealousy turns into evil envy.

Unlike jealousy, which focuses on possessing what you desire, envy focuses on taking something you desire away from the person who owns it. Envy is not just wanting what the other person has; envy is wanting the other person not to have it. No matter who is envied and who does the envying, the emotion always dismantles love.

Aristotle was the first to devote real thought to the problem of envy, calling it "the sin against the brother" — meaning that envy is felt most keenly by two people who are closely related. Whether it be by blood, by marriage, or by association, the toxic fumes of envy are most likely to appear when someone just like us succeeds. The newly graduated electrical engineer who is looking for work will envy a classmate's new job but have little problem with an actor friend who gets a plum role in a play. The closer a situation comes to matching our own identity, the

As rust corrupts iron, so envy corrupts man.   *Antisthenes* higher the stakes become and the more likely envy is to erupt. No wonder the classic love poem of 1 Corinthians says it so bluntly: Love does not envy. Why? Because the people we love the most are at risk for being the people we envy the most.

Let's face it. All of us — no matter how loving — carry a little envy. It's part of being human. Cross-cultural studies of jealousy and envy have found these emotions present in every culture. Moreover, they found that every person in a significant relationship experiences them from time to time. Hearing something good about someone just like us can deplete anyone of goodwill. But it's in these moments that love helps us rise above our petty self-centered concerns and celebrate another's success.

One of the best ways we have learned to guard against envy in our own marriage is to celebrate the good fortunes of others just like us. We make a concerted effort to genuinely rejoice with our friends who are rejoicing. In this way, we truly practice a love that "doesn't want what it doesn't have."

*E*nvy, like the worm, never runs but to the fairest fruit; like a cunning bloodhound, it singles out the fattest deer in the flock.
Francis Beaumont

---

1 Corinthians 13

The Message

If I speak with human eloquence and angelic ecstasy but don't love, I'm nothing but the creaking of a rusty gate.

If I speak God's Word with power, revealing all his mysteries and making everything plain as day, and if I have faith that says to a mountain, "Jump," and it jumps, but I don't love, I'm nothing.

If I give everything I own to the poor and even go to the stake to be burned as a martyr, but I don't love, I've gotten nowhere. So, no matter what I say, what I believe, and what I do, I'm bankrupt without love.

Love never gives up.

Love cares more for others than for self.

Love doesn't want what it doesn't have.

Love doesn't strut,

Doesn't have a swelled head,

Doesn't force itself on others,

Isn't always "me first,"

Doesn't fly off the handle,

Doesn't keep score of the sins of others,

Doesn't revel when others grovel,

Takes pleasure in the flowering of truth,

Puts up with anything,

Trusts God always,

Always looks for the best,

Never looks back,

But keeps going to the end.

Love never dies. Inspired speech will be over some day; praying in tongues will end; understanding will reach its limit. We know only a portion of the truth, and what we say about God is always incomplete. But when the Complete arrives, our incompletes will be canceled.

When I was an infant at my mother's breast, I gurgled and cooed like any infant. When I grew up, I left those infant ways for good.

We don't yet see things clearly. We're squinting in a fog, peering through a mist. But it won't be long before the weather clears and the sun shines bright! We'll see it all then, see it all as clearly as God sees us, knowing him directly just as he knows us!

But for right now, until that completeness, we have three things to do to lead us toward that consummation: Trust steadily in God, hope unswervingly, love extravagantly. And the best of the three is love.

Love Does Not Boast

[Love] doesn't say, "Look how wonderful I am,"
but "Look how great you are." — *Angela McCord*

We were sitting across the table from a couple we were just getting to know, enjoying Sunday brunch at a lovely restaurant, when the conversation turned to last year's Christmas.

"Didn't I buy you the dress you wanted at Nordstrom?" Carl asked.

"Well, you said — " Joanne started to respond.

"No, no. Just answer the question. Didn't I buy it for you?"

"Yes, but — "

"And didn't we go to your sister's house instead of taking the ski trip to Colorado I wanted?"

"Yes, and I was very grateful for that."

"So I gave you everything you asked for, right? Now tell them what you gave me."

A boaster and a liar are first cousins. *German proverb*

"Honey, this is stupid."

Joanne was right. This *was* stupid. You would have thought we'd ignited a tinderbox. It was embarrassing to everyone — except this poor woman's husband. Apparently she was used to it. As we walked to our car in the parking lot after the meal, Joanne told me (Leslie) that her husband "really likes to win."

We didn't talk about it there, but later that week Joanne called me for coffee and unpacked more of the story. Turns out her husband's bravado is his trademark. He boasts at work and at home. Anyone and everyone can be used by comparison to help him feel better about himself. If they granted degrees in boasting, he would have earned a Ph.D.

Boasting is a way of trying to look good when we suspect we are not good. It comes from an empty feeling that no one will appreciate us unless we show them how worthy we really are. It is an attempt to create an image of how we'd like others to see us. The problem for boasters is that images are fast fading. So their boasting becomes a compulsion to control other people's impressions. They don't trust things to take their course. They do everything in their power to help you see them in their best light. *Look at me. See what I've done. I deserve some recognition.* This is boasting.

A boaster is someone invited for dinner who proves that the night has a thousand I's. *Anonymous*

All of us, of course, want recognition. There's nothing wrong with needing to be noticed. It's our nature. But there is something wrong with boasting. When we try too hard to have people see us as better than we are, we hurt other people in the process. We fall into the proverbial trap of putting them down to push ourselves up.

Boasting always backfires. It brings a momentary sense of satisfaction, at best, but leaves an indelible mark of insecurity. Everyone knows the swagger of a show-off is paper-thin. You may think you are a person of good quality because you do, say, or buy the things a good person does. You may garner applause from the names you drop, the people you are seen with, the clubs you join, or the offices you hold, but boasting never buoys character. That's an inside job. All the boasting in the world will never bring a person closer to contentment. And a genuine lover loves most effectively from a contented heart. That's why love does not boast. That's why love doesn't say "Look how wonderful I am," but "Look how great you are."

I'm the best. I just haven't played yet.
Mohammed Ali on playing golf

1 Corinthians 13

Paraphrase by Angela McCord

If I go to language school and learn to speak a hundred different languages, preach to thousands all over the world, and lead all to Christ, but have hate in my heart in a silent war with my neighbor who's built his privacy fence on my side of the boundary line, my words are nothing except the screaming of a heavy metal rock band.

If I have a doctorate in theology, science, language arts, and literature and can raise mountains out of the dust of the plains, but am only concerned with the size of my paycheck, wardrobe, and house, it is as if I don't exist . . . have never existed.

If I give up a good salary opportunity to work in compassionate ministries, tithe ten percent, give the rest to the poor and eventually die for them, but only do it to get my name in the paper, and I lose sight of lost hungry souls, I certainly don't gain anything but lose my own soul.

Love walks the floor all night with a crying baby, smiles as she greets new visitors in Sunday school. She doesn't want what she doesn't have. She doesn't say, "Look how wonderful I am," but "Look how great you are." She doesn't snub anyone, isn't always looking in a mirror, and doesn't make a mental list for retribution when things don't go her way. She doesn't close herself in but opens her heart and makes herself vulnerable to others.

Love remains while the world crumbles around her.

While we live here on earth we can only see love in other people, a very imperfect reflection of the love of Christ, full of faults and human failures. But in heaven, we'll see Love in the form of Jesus. And now I can show love in part—full of my own humanity, but *then* I can love perfectly, even as I am completely loved.

The only things that are really important are faith in God, hope for the future, and love from God for every man. But you cannot have faith or hope until you first understand and demonstrate love.

I can work with the poor like Mother Teresa, write literature like C. S. Lewis, sing like Sandi Patti, move people like Gloria Gaither, preach like Billy Graham, have spiritual insight like James Dobson, be a great leader like Martin Luther King, Jr., and a martyr like Ghandi, but until I love like Jesus my soul is lost.

Love Is Not Proud

Love . . . is [not] haughty in mind. — *J. Oswald Sanders*

I'm not going to have a daughter of mine married on Goodyear tires."

Harvey Firestone said this to one of his managers in Akron, Ohio, the day his daughter, Martha, was getting married to Edsel Ford's son, William. In the tradition of the Ford family, the groom's party drove from Detroit in a small fleet of new Lincolns, which were duly parked in the Firestone executive garage. That's when the manager noticed that all the Lincolns of the Ford party were mounted with Goodyear tires and reported the news to Harvey Firestone.

"Jack up all the Lincolns," Harvey told the manager, "take off the Goodyears, and put on ours. I want Martha to be married in style."

Harvey Firestone not only took pride in his daughter's marriage, he took pride in his product. Anything wrong with that? We don't think so. Pride is a healthy

Proud people breed sad sorrows for themselves. *Emily Brontë*

by-product of work well done. Who doesn't want to do something you can be proud of? But if pride can be good why does Paul tell us love is not proud?

The answer is found in understanding the kind of pride Paul is talking about. Pride comes in two forms. And one of them brings certain death to love. This lethal pride is nurtured by vanity and promoted by arrogance. It is spiritually bankrupt and causes you to puff yourself up. It refuses God's help, never praying for grace, pleading for mercy, or giving thanks to God. It is arrogance in the vertical direction and is the root of all evil. English journalist Daniel Defoe calls this kind of pride "the first peer and president of hell."

Arrogant pride — the kind that refuses to let God be God — is certain to contaminate love and marriage. Why? Those who rely only on their own resources eventually become a law unto themselves and exploit others in the process. Pride depletes them of humility. It keeps them from asking for help and prevents them from acknowledging the help they received anyway. The arrogance of this pride is focused on one question: *What can I get out of this relationship?* It compels us to consider only our own needs and causes us to shed mercy and compassion. When arrogance creeps into our marriage, we lose

*T*he core of pride is self-rejection. *Eric Hoffer*

respect for our partner and eventually ourselves. *I don't need you*, says this kind of pride. *I'm better than you.*

So let's be clear on these two kinds of pride. Unhealthy pride is bankrupt of love. It reeks of arrogance and self-consumption. It is its own mirror, reflecting whatever image it desires. It is "haughty in mind."

Healthy pride, on the other hand, is grounded in reality and centered on truth. It revels in the joy of goodness for goodness' sake — not as a means for self-promotion. This kind of pride in one's work or in a partner's accomplishments balances satisfaction and sufficiency with thanksgiving and humility. It admits weakness and claims strength at the same time. Healthy pride has a steady ego that is able to laugh at its own foibles. Healthy pride keeps its eyes off other people's faults and is content to walk humbly alongside them.

Humility is highest when it stoops. *Channing Pollock*

1 Corinthians 13

Translation by J. Oswald Sanders

If I speak with the tongues of the angels above
or the tongues of the seers, but am lacking in love
my words are all hollow, nor will they surpass
the clatter of cymbals, the clanging of brass.
If I see as a prophet and know as a sage
and read the occult as an obvious page,
and the might of my faith can a mountain remove,
with it all I am nothing if I have not love.
If I give to the poor all the wealth I have earned
and if as a martyr my body is burned
and love does not move to the gift or the pain,
they profit me nothing, my bounties are vain.
Love suffereth long, and is endlessly kind;
Love envieth not nor is haughty in mind;
Love never is harsh; love seeks not her own;
and a grudge and revenge to love are unknown.
Love praises no evil, is true as the day;
love heareth, believeth, and hopeth for aye.
Though knowledge may cease, and though
   prophecies pale,

love never, no never, no never shall fail.
Now ever abideth the faith of the free,
and high hope, and love these dominant three;
but greatest and happiest, soaring above
all glories, all joys, and all powers is love.

Love Is Not Rude

Love . . . is not . . . unmannerly. — *Berkeley Version*

$\mathcal{T}$he past two decades have revealed more about what it takes to make love last than ever before. "Being in love," it turns out, is a very poor predictor of which couples will be married years down the road. Far more important to the survival of a marriage, research shows, is how well couples handle conflict. Some husbands or wives mistake calmness and quiet for marital harmony and go out of their way to smooth over differences or ignore them altogether. They don't want to make waves, or even ripples. Other husbands or wives do just the opposite. Something, almost anything, can set them off, and they lambaste their partner without restraint. While both styles of handling conflict are unhealthy, it is the latter that concerns experts the most. It is an unmannerly, discourteous, and aggressive style guaranteed to be lethal to love.

$\mathcal{R}$udeness is the weak man's imitation of strength.   *Eric Hoffer*

When a conflict degenerates to hurling insults, researchers raise a red flag and call it contempt. It's a sign that a spouse is intentionally trying to hurt his partner. Name-calling, hostile humor, and mockery are the weapons of choice. And stressed-out, dual-career couples today who have more to negotiate than ever are especially prone to this calamity. That's why Paul's seemingly obvious statement is so critical for contemporary couples. Love is not rude. Don't pass too quickly over this little sentence. It just may hold the key to helping you fight a good fight — one that steers clear of contempt.

Jennifer Crocker and Ian Schwarts have uncovered the primary motivator of rude behavior, and you can probably guess what it is. These researches wanted to know for sure if and how low self-esteem causes contempt. To find answers to their questions, Crocker and Schwarts asked forty-two college students to complete a questionnaire evaluating their self-esteem.* Then students were arbitrarily divided into two groups, labeled "alphas" and "betas," by the researchers. All the students were asked to indicate their expectations regarding the personality of each person in both groups, rating them on desirable and undesirable characteristics.

---

*Jennifer Crocker and Ian Schwarts, *Personality and Social Psychology Bulletin* 11, no. 4 (1986).

A cynic can chill and dishearten with a single word.
Ralph Waldo Emerson

What did the alphas have to say about the betas and vice versa? Despite the fact that these students had never met, their opinions of each other often were colored by their self-esteem. Individuals with high self-esteem rated both groups more favorably than did those whose self-esteem was low. Interestingly, those with low self-esteem were not at all discriminating: While they showed strong prejudice toward those in the other group, they did not value members of their own group any more highly. Crocker and Schwarts conclude, "Low self-esteem individuals seem to have a generally negative view of themselves, their own group, other groups, and perhaps the world."

The same is true in marriage. The husband or wife who feels empty on the inside, whose self-worth and dignity have all but vanished, will eventually resort to rude behavior, tearing down their partner, in a last-ditch effort to build themselves up. And when this tactic becomes a two-way street, which it often does, with both partners acting uncivil, they separate themselves from the person who could help them the most. So pay attention to Paul's simple statement and never forget that love is not unmannerly.

False words are not only evil in themselves, but they infect the soul with evil. *Socrates*

1 Corinthians 13

Berkeley Version

I will show you a course that runs higher.

Even though I speak in every human and angelic language and have no love, I am as noisy brass or a loud-sounding cymbal. And although I have prophetic gift and see through every secret and through all that may be known, and have sufficient faith for the removal of mountains, but I have no love, I am useless. And though I give all my belongings for nourishment (to the needy) and surrender my body to be burned, but I have no love, I am not in the least benefited.

Love endures long and is kind; love is not jealous; love is not for display; it is not conceited or unmannerly; it is neither self-seeking nor irritable, nor does it take account of a suffered wrong. It takes no pleasure in injustice, but it sides happily with truth. It covers up everything, has unquenchable faith, hopes under all circumstances, endures without limit.

Love never fades out. As for prophesyings, they shall be rendered useless; as for tongues, they shall cease; as for knowledge, it shall lose its meaning. For our knowledge is fragmentary and so is our prophesying. But when the total ensues then the fragmentary becomes antiquated.

When I was a child I talked as a child; I entertained child interests; I reasoned like a child; but on becoming a man I am through with childish ways. For now we see indistinctly in a mirror; but then face to face. Now we know partly, but then we shall understand as completely as we are understood.

There remain, then, faith, hope, love, these three; but the greatest of these is love.

Love Is Not Self-Seeking

Love . . . does not . . . try to get things for itself.
— *Cotton Patch Version*

*Y*ou're going to vacuum before they get here, right?"
Leslie asked in an anxious tone as we were pulling
into the garage.

"I've got it under control," I murmured.

We jumped out of the car, each grabbed an armful
of groceries, and hurried toward the kitchen. "I'll take
care of these groceries so you can get started on the vacu-
uming," Leslie said. The tension was rising because in
less than an hour, two other couples would be at our
doorstep expecting a dinner party. "Don't forget to light
the candles and turn on the music before they get here,"
Leslie hollered from the kitchen. I heard what she said
but didn't reply as I walked into my study to look
through some "urgent" mail.

Only a couple of minutes passed, it seemed to me,
when Leslie came into my study and in exasperation
asked, "What are you doing?"

*H*owever it is debased or misinterpreted, love is a
redemptive feature. . . .

"Reading my mail," I responded defensively and with the best look of confusion I could put on my face. She didn't buy it. "Don't worry," I said, "I'll take care of the other stuff."

Leslie sighed and left the room. Five minutes later I heard the sound of the vacuum in the living room. *I'm almost done here, and then I'll go in and help her*, I said to myself. Ten minutes later the vacuum stopped. I bolted from my chair and walked to the living room. "I thought I was going to do this," I said to Leslie.

"So did I," she replied.

We've all weaseled our way out of somebody's "to do" list at one time or another, haven't we? After all, we've worked hard, we're tired, busy, preoccupied, maxed-out, whatever. There are a dozen reasons we use to justify one of the deadliest saboteurs of love: self-seeking. It lurks just beneath the surface whenever we are tired and there's a household chore to be done or an errand to be run. That's when we pretend we don't notice the chore, or we "forget" about the task, hoping somebody else will take over so we don't have to. That's when our self-centered side shows up.

Like it or not, all of us are selfish. It's a quality that saturates the human soul. Yet this simple sentence from 1 Corinthians — "love is not self-seeking" — barely elicits more than a sanctimonious nod of agreement from most

... To focus on one individual so that their desires become superior to yours is a very cleansing experience. *Jeanette Winterson*

of us. *Of course love isn't selfish*, we think to ourselves, *and all those selfish people out there need to understand this*.

Truth is, each and every one of us needs to contemplate this simple sentence and seriously reflect upon how our own selfish nature subtly seeps into the crevices of all our relationships. This sentence calls us to take a hard look in the mirror and recognize just how self-seeking we "loving" people can be.

I (Leslie) am the first to admit I tend to look out for my own interest. I can selfishly hoard my husband's time. I can whine and complain to Les about his busy schedule but never consider adjusting my own calendar for his benefit. Or I might think nothing of spending extravagantly on a luncheon with one of my girlfriends and later snip at Les for indulging himself with another computer gadget he "doesn't need." In big and small ways we all squirrel away money, energy, and time for our own advantage, never realizing we are squandering countless acts of love.

Neither of us is a selfless saint, not by a long shot. But we've both learned that love sets aside self-seeking to build the kind of relationship we long for. Over time, we've learned that the more frequently we seek each other's needs and those around us — through sacrifice and service — the more power love has to fill our lives.

The only purpose for seeking our selves is to become better at seeking others. *Lewis B. Smedes*

1 Corinthians 13

Cotton Patch Version

*A*nd I want to show you the greatest way of all:

Though I speak with the tongues of men and of angels, but have no love, I am a hollow-sounding horn or a nerve-wracking rattle. And though I have the ability to preach, and know all the secrets and all the slogans, and though I have sufficient faith to move a mountain, but have no love, I am nothing. Even though I renounce all my possessions, and give my body as a flaming sacrifice, but have no love, I accomplish exactly nothing. Love is long-suffering and kind. Love is not envious, nor does it strut and brag. It does not act up, nor try to get things for itself. It pitches no tantrums, keeps no books on insults or injuries, sees no fun in wickedness, but rejoices when truth prevails. Love is all-embracing, all-trusting, all-hoping, all-enduring. Love never quits. As for sermons, they shall be silenced; as for oratory, it shall cease; as for knowledge, it will vanish. For our knowledge is immature, and our preaching is immature; but when that which is mature arrives, it supersedes the immature. For example, when I was a child, I was talking like a child, thinking like a child, acting like a child, but when I became an adult, I outgrew my childish ways. So, on the childish level [i.e., *without love*] we look at one another in a trick mirror, but on the adult level [i.e., *with love*] we see face to face; as a child [i.e., *without love*] I understand immaturely, but as an adult [i.e., *with love*] I'll understand just as I'll be understood. Now these three things endure: faith, hope and love; but the greatest of all is love. Seek diligently for love.

Love Is Not Easily Angered

Love ... is not quickly made angry.
— *Basic Bible Translation*

For the most part, Rick was as kind and mild-mannered a person as you'd ever want to meet. He was a dedicated husband and father, made a decent living, and was a devoted churchgoer. But every once in a while, as his teenage daughter put it, Rick would simply "lose it." He would get so frustrated with something or someone and erupt in an explosion of anger. One day, for example, Rick pulled into his driveway after a full day of work and discovered a couple of stray toys his nine-year-old son had absentmindedly left there. Time and again, Rick had asked Jimmy to keep his toys off the driveway but, like most children, the boy forgot.

Anger blows out the lamp of the mind.   *Robert Green Ingersoll*

Seeing his son's bicycle lying on its side, obstructing his path to the garage, Rick sat in his car and laid on the horn. He honked for nearly half a minute, and the only response he got was a strange look from one of his neighbors. Seething with anger, Rick threw his car into reverse, backed up five feet, screeched his brakes, and left the car in a huff. He picked up the bike and threw it angrily onto the sidewalk.

When Rick came into the house, he walked briskly past his wife who by this time was hanging up from her phone conversation and watching the whole scene from the kitchen window. "What's going on out there?" she innocently asked. Rick said nothing. He stomped into his den, slamming the door behind him while his wife stood dumbfounded outside the door. A few minutes later, she softly knocked and heard him grumble a reply to enter. She stuck her head inside, and said, "Jimmy needs a ride to his scout meeting, and you have a church board meeting tonight. Can you take him with you?" He sheepishly nodded his answer, and the evening proceeded like nothing unusual had ever happened.

There is no emotion that puts the brakes on love more abruptly than anger, and everyone knows it. Sometimes, as in Rick's case, our outbursts of anger even embarrass us. But that hasn't stopped us.

Anger is one of the sinews of the soul; he that wants it hath a maimed mind. *Thomas Fuller*

In an attempt to cope with angry feelings that don't seem so loving, well-meaning people have approached the emotion with a variety of perspectives. Some people deal with their anger by denying it. They say they are weary, uptight, nervous, distraught, or overwhelmed. But anger by any other name is still anger.

Others try, unsuccessfully, to suppress angry feelings. Maybe if they don't talk, the reasoning goes, they won't be angry. The problem with this approach is that suppressed anger has a high rate of resurrection. Some try to spiritualize anger. They like to cling to "righteous" anger as a defense for their "unrighteous" behavior. Which basically translates into the idea that "my anger is righteous and yours is not!"

A growing number of people flaunt their anger. "This is the way God made me, and I can't help it; so don't be surprised if you push me too far. I'll explode!"

Let's be honest. All of us at some time have erupted with irrational anger. Each of us has a boiling point. If pushed far enough, everyone will lash out. It's only human. This fact is inferred in this line from 1 Corinthians. It does not say love never gets angry. It says love does not get angry very easily. In other words, a loving person can be provoked to anger, but not without significant effort.

If you are patient in one moment of anger, you will escape a hundred days of sorrow.   *Chinese proverb*

A loving person also knows how to time his anger. As Aristotle put it: "Anybody can become angry — that is easy; but to be angry with the right person, and to the right degree, and at the right time, and for the right purpose, and in the right way — that is not within everybody's power and is not easy."

Love does not try to deny anger, suppress it, spiritualize it, or flaunt it. No. In the midst of a million inevitable irritants of life, love puts a long fuse on anger. How? By dethroning our obsession with self-satisfactions. As we focus less exclusively on ourselves, love raises our threshold for anger by reducing our level of irritability. That's what keeps anger at bay. The more we concern ourselves with other people's needs, the more power we exercise over anger. That's why love is not *easily* angered.

A gentle answer turns away wrath, but a harsh word stirs up anger. *Proverbs 15:1*

1 Corinthians 13

Basic Bible Translation

I am pointing out to you an even better way.

If I make use of the tongues of men and of angels, and have not love, I am like sounding brass, or a loud-tongued bell. And if I have a prophet's power, and have knowledge of all secret things; and if I have all faith, by which mountains may be moved from their place, but have not love, I am nothing.

And if I give all my goods to the poor, and if I give my body to be burned, but have not love, it is of no profit to me.

Love is never tired of waiting; love is kind; love has no envy; love has no high opinion of itself, love has no pride;

Love's ways are ever fair, it takes no thought for itself; it is not quickly made angry, it takes no account of evil;

It takes no pleasure in wrongdoing, but has joy in what is true;

Love has the power of undergoing all things, having faith in all things, hoping all things.

Though the prophet's word may come to an end, tongues come to nothing, and knowledge have no more value, love has no end.

For our knowledge is only in part, and the prophet's word gives only a part of what is true:

But when that which is complete is come, then that which is in part will be no longer necessary.

When I was a child, I made use of a child's language, I had a child's feelings and a child's thoughts: now that I am a man, I have put away the things of a child.

For now we see things in a glass, darkly; but then face to face: now my knowledge is in part; then it will be complete, even as God's knowledge of me.

But now we still have faith, hope, love, these three; and the greatest of these is love.

Love Keeps No Record of Wrongs

Love ... does not brood over injury.
— *New American Bible*

We were having lunch with one of the world's most renowned marriage experts, Dr. John Gottman of the University of Washington, when we began talking about couples who "kitchen sink." This was John's way of describing how some tumultuous couples toss in every conceivable negative thing you can imagine when a conflict erupts: "You never called to say you were going to be late, on top of never even making a restaurant reservation. What's more, you didn't pick up the dry cleaning last week, and you left your dirty laundry all over the bedroom."

Once a woman has forgiven her man, she must not reheat his sins for breakfast. *Marlene Dietrich*

When one partner has temporarily exhausted their laundry list of offenses, the other one will soon retaliate: "Apparently you don't remember talking on the phone for more than an hour so I couldn't get through to you. Just like you did last week and the week before. And I wouldn't have to make a restaurant reservation if we ever had a hot meal on the table like you keep promising."

This painful Ping-Pong match of hurling offenses goes on ad nauseam for some warring couples. They seem to be armed and ready with an endless list of ways the other person has hurt, harmed, and wronged them.

At the root of every "record of wrong" is resentment. The memory of past pain becomes a present injustice as we replay it over and over in our mind. Yesterday's hurts are nurtured by today's frustration. We soak in them. We don't let them rest. And peace of mind — not to mention peace with our partner — is the price we pay for keeping resentment alive. So why do we do it? Why do we keep score? Why do we prolong our pain? The answer is found in false hope. We keep a record of wrongs because we believe we will get our just rewards if we show how bad the other person has been. If we reveal how out of kilter the scales of marital justice are, we believe our spouse will see the truth and feel compelled to rectify the imbalance. Add to that our feeling of being a

Would not love see returning penitence afar off, and fall on its neck and kiss it? George Eliot

decent person who was wrongly hurt, and you have all you need for resentment to fester.

The sad truth is that resentment never rights a wrong. No matter how compelling, a record of wrongs only drives the offender farther from your circle of love. It is the rare and heroic case where broadcasting faults brings a person to repentance. More likely, resentment builds a barrier that hardens our hopeful hearts, as well as the heart of the one we love — or used to.

So, love does not brood over injuries. It keeps no record of wrongs because it cannot survive in doing so. Love knows that keeping track of tit for tat never brings equilibrium to an out-of-balance relationship. Love understands that wrongs are a part of life and that no record can ever right them. Instead, the power of love is found in letting go of our record keeping. It loosens our grip on past pain and drives us to a fresh start. Love lets the history die and gives birth to a new beginning. It surrenders the compulsion to clear up every misunderstanding and lets the ledgers stay unbalanced. Love prefers to let forgiveness heal former hurts so that we can focus on the future.

Of course, to keep no record of wrongs — to let loose our list of painful memories — is one of the toughest things any human being could ever do. But love holds the power to do just that.

We pardon to the extent that we love.
François, Duc de La Rochefoucauld

1 Corinthians 13

New American Bible

*B*ut I shall show you a still more excellent way.

If I speak in human and angelic tongues, but do not have love, I am a resounding gong or a clashing cymbal. And if I have the gift of prophecy, and comprehend all mysteries and all knowledge; if I have all faith so as to move mountains, but do not have love, I am nothing. If I give away everything I own, and if I hand my body over so that I may boast, but do not have love, I gain nothing.

Love is patient, love is kind. It is not jealous, [love] is not pompous, it is not inflated, it is not rude, it does not seek its own interests, it is not quick-tempered, it does not brood over injury, it does not rejoice over wrongdoing but rejoices with the truth. It bears all things, believes all things, hopes all things, endures all things.

Love never fails. If there are prophecies, they will be brought to nothing; if tongues, they will cease; if knowledge, it will be brought to nothing. For we know partially and we prophesy partially, but when the perfect comes, the partial will pass away. When I was a child, I used to talk as a child, think as a child, reason as a child; when I became a man, I put aside childish things. At present we see indistinctly, as in a mirror, but then face to face. At present I know partially; then I shall know fully as I am fully known. So faith, hope, love remain, these three; but the greatest of these is love.

Love Rejoices with the Truth

She has no sympathy with deceit, but has full sympathy
with truth. — *Twentieth Century New Testament*

*N*icole loved Lew. There was no mistaking that.
High school sweethearts and married for nearly
fifteen years, they were each other's soul mates. But
something was amiss. In spite of their connection,
Nicole felt compelled to schedule an appointment and
find her way to our counseling office.

"I'm not sure," Nicole softly confessed, "but I'm
afraid Lew is losing interest in me and our marriage."

"What makes you suspicious?"

"Well, he's drinking again and rarely wants to make
love."

"He's drinking again?" Les blurted out.

"Well, he's always liked to drink." Nicole went on to
innocently unravel a classic case of an alcoholic husband.

*T*ruth indeed rather alleviates than hurts, and will always bear up
against falsehood, as oil does above water.   *Miguel de Cervantes*

A little more probing revealed plenty of good reasons for Nicole's suspicion, if not an open-and-closed case of marital deceit.

"What does Lew say when you confront him?"

"Oh, I've never confronted Lew," Nicole said with surprise. "I've just tried to be a loving spouse. You know, love him in spite of his weaknesses."

We both winced as Nicole laid out a picture of her marriage — a picture that was far from pretty. This marriage was no fairy tale. We learned that Nicole not only never stood up to Lew about his alcoholism, but she routinely made excuses to herself and others for his bad behavior. For years she covered up his problem in the name of being a good wife.

It doesn't take a therapist to see the problem in this marriage. Nicole, like many of us who long for genuine intimacy in our marriage, was blind to the very thing that kept intimacy from developing. Nicole, in her attempt to be loving, was unable to see the truth. And she was missing out on authentic love because of it.

Love is *not* blind. Love takes a good, hard look at reality. That's why love rejoices with the truth. Truth keeps love honest, reminding it that an untrustworthy person who is loved is still untrustworthy. Real love, the kind Paul is writing about, does not live in an idealistic fairy tale. It doesn't sweep unpleasant bits of reality

It takes two to speak the truth — one to speak and another to hear. Henry David Thoreau

under the rug. No. Love is open-eyed to what's really going on. It allows us to recognize the presence of evil when all we want to see is good. Sure, love softens the jagged corners of hard truths. It guards against the all-too-frequent brutality of reality. But love never loses sight of the way things really are.

Love and truth have a give-and-take relationship. Just as truth keeps love honest, so does love keep truth grounded in reality. Without love, truth's obsession with facts shapes those facts into unforgiving weapons. A fact, drawn out of context, turns into a lie. It may be a fact that your partner has committed a sensational sin. But love knows the difference between falling into sin and planning one's life around it. Love, not hiding from the truth, still seeks a path toward redemption. Love drives us to will only good for persons and thus forces us to see anything that hurts them needlessly as an intolerable evil.

Nicole and Lew, in time, discovered how love rejoices with the triumph of truth. Lew still fights his demons, but not alone. Nicole, fully aware of her husband's real struggles, helps hold him accountable. She replaced her idealistic dream with a realistic vision. And they are both rejoicing in their rebuilt love.

*T*ruth is tough. It will not break, like a bubble, at a touch; nay, you may kick it about all day like a football, and it will be round and full at evening. *Oliver Wendell Holmes Sr.*

1 Corinthians 13

Twentieth Century New Testament

I go on to show you a way beyond all comparison the best.

If I speak in the "tongues" of men—aye, and of angels, too—but am without Love, I have become mere echoing brass, or a clanging cymbal! Even if I have the "prophetic" gift and know all secret truths and possess all knowledge, or even if I have such perfect faith as to be able to move mountains, but am without Love, I am nothing! If I give all that I possess to feed the hungry, and even if (to say what is boastful) I sacrifice my body, but am without Love, I am none the better!

Love is long-suffering and kind. Love is never envious, never boastful, never conceited, never behaves unbecomingly. She is not self-seeking, not easily provoked, *nor does she reckon up her wrongs*. She has no sympathy with deceit, but has full sympathy with truth. She is proof against all things, always trustful, always hopeful, always patient.

Love never dies. Are there "prophetic" gifts?—they will be cast aside. Are there "tongues"?—they will cease.

Is there knowledge? —it will be cast aside. Our knowledge is incomplete, and our prophesying incomplete, but as soon as Perfection has come, what is incomplete will be cast aside. When I was a child, I talked like a child, thought like a child, reasoned like a child; now that I am a man, I have cast childish ways aside. As yet we see things dimly, reflected in a mirror, but then—face to face! As yet my knowledge is incomplete, but then it will be as full as God's knowledge of me is now. So then Faith, Hope, and Love last on—only these three—and of them the greatest is Love.

$\mathcal{L}$ove $\mathcal{A}$lways $\mathcal{P}$rotects

Love ... always protects.
—*New International Reader's Version*

$\mathcal{L}$ast summer we were speaking in Washington, D.C., at a national marriage conference. With two hours of unstructured time one afternoon, we caught a cab and made our way to the Smithsonian Institute to view one of our nation's most prized documents, the Declaration of Independence.

We stood in a long line for a brief look at this historical treasure. Before we reached the viewing area in front of the bulletproof glass I noticed that almost everyone said something to the guard who stood nearby. When our turn came, I studied the document for a few moments and then turned to the guard myself. "It looks like almost everyone makes a comment or asks a question of you before leaving," I said. "What question do you hear the most?"

The guard didn't pause. "Everyone," he said, "wants to know how the Declaration of Independence is protected."

$\mathcal{I}$mmature love says: "I love you because I need you." Mature love says: "I need you because I love you." *Erich Fromm*

He proceeded to tell us how each night it is mechanically transported into a huge vault sunk deep beneath the ground of the museum.

As we caught our return cab back to the conference, Leslie mused, "It's so true. We want to be sure the things we love are safe and sound." Paul makes the point as plain as possible: "Love always protects."

But can it really? Can love safeguard your husband or wife from pain? Not really. To guarantee such a promise is absurd. But love can protect the one you love from walking in pain alone. In fact, some of life's most piercing pain comes from not having a companion who walks with us. The Latin origins of *protect* literally mean to cover over or walk in front of. And that's just how love's power to protect works. It moves us to carry our partner's pain as if it were our own. It compels us to cover our partner with companionship.

Consider the painful times in your own life. Didn't the most dramatic relief come when someone entered your situation with you and helped you carry your burden? This person literally protected you from further pain by carrying some of it away. Because of his or her love, your pain became less difficult to bear. And to take it a step further, love not only protects us by reducing our pain, it protects us by enabling healing to begin once the pain is present. In other words, love protects us from let-

*S*ecurity comes when I'm in love with somebody who loves me back. *Shelley Winters*

ting an emotional wound fester with anger and resentment. Love knows how to keep its mouth shut and just listen. Love creates a safe place to talk it out and thus protects us from doing something foolish.

Love keeps us safe by its very nature. It is a foolproof security system. It wraps us in acceptance and guards us in its embrace. When we are loved — when we are wanted, claimed, and enjoyed by another — nothing can hurt us to the core. Because love always protects.

We are each of us angels with only one wing. And we can only fly embracing each other. *Luciano de Cresenzo*

1 Corinthians 13

New International Reader's Version

And now I will show you the best way of all.

Suppose I speak in the languages of human beings and of angels. If I don't have love, I am only a loud gong or a noisy cymbal. Suppose I have the gift of prophecy. Suppose I can understand all the secret things of God and know everything about him. And suppose I have enough faith to move mountains. If I don't have love, I am nothing at all. Suppose I give everything I have to poor people. And suppose I give my body to be burned. If I don't have love, I get nothing at all.

Love is patient. Love is kind. It does not want what belongs to others. It does not brag. It is not proud. It is not rude. It does not look out for its own interests. It does not easily become angry. It does not keep track of other people's wrongs.

Love is not happy with evil. But it is full of joy when the truth is spoken. It always protects. It always trusts. It always hopes. It never gives up.

Love never fails. But prophecy will pass away. Speaking in languages that had not been known before will end. And knowledge will pass away.

What we know now is not complete. What we prophesy now is not perfect. But when what is perfect comes, the things that are not perfect will pass away.

When I was a child, I talked like a child. I thought like a child. I had the understanding of a child. When I became an adult, I put childish ways behind me.

Now we see only a dim likeness of things. It is as if we were seeing them in a mirror. But someday we will see clearly. We will see face to face. What I know now is not complete. But someday I will know completely, just as God knows me completely.

The three most important things to have are faith, hope and love. But the greatest of them is love.

Love Always Trusts

Love . . . is completely trusting. — *William Barclay*

*M*yrle is one of the most suspicious people we know, and for good reason. He's been a detective with the Seattle Police Department for nearly thirty years. The things you and I would barely notice, how someone parks their car or the stain on their tie, for example, Myrle examines to reveal volumes about their activities. On more than one occasion when we've been riding with Myrle in his unmarked vehicle he's noticed something "peculiar." He slows down, circles the block, or even gets out on foot to ease his suspicions. Like we said, Myrle is one of the most suspicious people we know — until he's with Dorothy.

Myrle and Dorothy have been married as long as he's been a cop, and you don't have to be around them very long before you realize he'd trust Dorothy with his life. Why? Because love always trusts. Love sets aside

*I*t is impossible to go through life without trust: that is to be imprisoned in the worst cell of all, oneself. *Graham Greene*

suspicions and doubt. It lets down its guard and becomes somewhat careless.

You might even say that love can make you gullible. Not that gullibility is a sign of love. People who believe the stories in grocery store tabloids and are sure every salesperson is sincere are not necessarily more loving. But love can make even the most cynical person totally trusting. Part of love's power is its ability to move us to trust the one we love.

That's what Paul is driving at with this statement. It's important to realize he's not setting forth a mandate or law that says loving people must always trust everyone. He's not proclaiming a duty. Paul is speaking of love's impulse. He's talking about how love moves us to trust the one we love. He's celebrating the fact that love creates a place where we can relax, let down our guard, and confide in the safety of someone else. He's highlighting the joy love finds in not having to calculate odds and worry about being cheated.

On some occasions wisdom will tell us to hold back love's impulse to trust. But the fact remains that love pushes us to believe in the goodness of another. Perhaps that's what Scottish novelist and poet George MacDonald was pondering when he said, "To be trusted is a greater compliment than to be loved." If you have won someone's trust, you can be assured they love you.

To love at all is to be vulnerable.   *C. S. Lewis*

How can love be so completely trusting, you may wonder. Because it has nothing to lose. It is in the business of giving itself away. Love only has eyes for another person's needs, so in a sense, love can't be robbed. Sure it risks being deceived and hurt, but love's power is found in the very act of taking this vulnerable risk. Love takes an uncalculated chance every time it walks the extra mile. But it does not do so with the risk in mind. Love doesn't measure the distance beforehand. If love feels a little naive it is not for lack of experience with people, but because love does not bother to calculate what it might lose.

Love's not too careful. Why? Because when love is completely trusting, it is at peace to love all the more.

The highest compact we can make with our fellow is — "Let there be truth between us two forevermore." *Ralph Waldo Emerson*

1 Corinthians 13

Translation by William Barclay

I show you still a more excellent way.

I may speak with the tongues of men and of angels, but if I have not love, I am become no better than echoing brass or a clanging cymbal. I may have the gift of prophecy, I may understand all sacred secrets and all knowledge. I may have faith enough to remove mountains, but if I have not love I am nothing. I may dole out all that I have, I may surrender my body that I may be burned, but if I have not love it is no good to me.

Love is patient; love is kind; love knows no envy; love is no braggart; it is not inflated with its own importance; it does not behave gracelessly; it does not insist on its own rights; it never flies into a temper; it does not store up the memory of any wrong it has received; it finds no pleasure in evil-doing; it rejoices with the truth; it can endure anything; it is completely trusting; it never ceases to hope; it bears everything with triumphant fortitude.

Love never fails. Whatever prophecies there are, they will vanish away. Whatever tongues there are, they will cease. Whatever knowledge we have, it will pass away. It is only part of the truth that we know now and only part of the truth that we can forthtell to others. But when that which is complete shall come, that which is incomplete will vanish away. When I was a child I used to speak like a child; I used to think like a child; I used to reason like a child. When I became a man I put an end to childish things. Now we see only reflections in a mirror which leaves us with nothing but riddles to solve, but then we shall see face to face. Now I know in part; but then I will know even as I am now. Now faith, hope, love remain — these three: but the greatest of these is love.

Love Always Hopes

Love knows . . . no fading of its hope; it can
outlast anything. — *J. B. Phillips*

On a trip to London with two other couples we sometimes vacation with, we visited the British Museum
where we discovered an unusual painting called *Hope*.
On the background of this canvas were the familiar out-
lines of the continents and oceans of planet Earth. In
the foreground was a beautiful woman seated at a harp.
Nearly all of the harp's strings dangled helplessly from
the top of the harp or lay uselessly on the lap of the
woman's dress. Only one string remained taut.

One of our friends commented on how little of the
harp was still intact and said, "I wonder why they call the
painting *Hope*?" The answer was clear to me. Hope is the
song of a broken instrument — knowing that if you pluck
that one string, you can still have music.

Hope is what empowers us to draw on our reservoir
of determination and make a commitment to improve our

*W*hoso loves believes the impossible. *Elizabeth Barrett Browning*

circumstances. Hope transforms. That's why love always hopes.

Every couple about to be married, whether they admit it or not, harbors dreams of a "perfect" life together. Many newlyweds have told us how "lucky" they felt on their wedding day to have met someone who understands them, who shares their likes and dislikes, and who is so compatible with them.

Yet, no matter how ideally suited they are, at some point every husband and wife realize that theirs is not a perfect match. They become aware that they do not always agree, that they do not think, feel, and behave in exactly the same manner, that merging their two personalities and preferences and backgrounds is much more difficult than they ever expected. Their bubble is burst, and they are faced with a choice. They can give up hope and resign themselves to living in a miserable marriage. Or they can draw on the power of love to keep hope alive as they accept the fact that marriages can never be perfect because people are not perfect.

Being human, every bride and groom have faults as well as virtues. We are at times gloomy, cranky, selfish, or unreasonable. We are a mixture of generous, altruistic feelings combined with self-seeking aims, petty vanities, and overweening ambitions. Marriage is an alloy of gold and tin. If we expect more than this, we are doomed to disap-

The way we conceive the future sculpts the present, gives contour and tone to nearly every action and thought through the day. If our sense of future is weak, we live listlessly. *Eugene Peterson*

pointment. Without hope, marriage becomes a living hell. Dante tells us that the sign that hangs over the entrance of hell reads, "Abandon hope, ye who enter here."

That's why love always hopes, even in some of the most hopeless situations. An alcoholic husband who has turned his wife's everyday life into a hellish nightmare strains hope, but yet it can survive. A wife who has secretly maxed out every credit card and driven her husband into debt without his knowledge pushes the limits of hope, but yet it can live. As long as hope survives so does a glimmer of love. Hope enables love to coexist with life's inevitable pain. As J. B. Phillips underscores in his translation of Paul's poem: "Love knows no fading of this hope; it can outlast anything."

Again, that's why love always hopes — because hope keeps love alive.

*W*e cannot think, feel, will, or act without the perception of a goal. *Alfred Adler*

1 Corinthians 13

Translation by J. B. Phillips

*I*f I speak with the eloquence of men and of angels, but have no love, I become no more than blaring brass or crashing cymbal. If I have the gift of foretelling the future and hold in my mind not only all human knowledge but the very secrets of God, and if I also have that absolute faith which can move mountains, but have no love, I amount to nothing at all. If I dispose of all that I possess, yes, even if I give my own body to be burned, but have no love, I achieve precisely nothing

This love of which I speak is slow to lose patience — it looks for a way of being constructive. It is not possessive: it is neither anxious to impress nor does it cherish inflated ideas of its own importance.

Love has good manners and does not pursue selfish advantage. It is not touchy. It does not keep account of evil or gloat over the wickedness of other people. On the contrary, it is glad with all good men when Truth prevails.

Love knows no limit to its endurance, no end to its trust, no fading of its hope; it can outlast anything. It is, in fact, the one thing that still stands when all else has fallen.

For if there are prophecies they will be fulfilled and done with, if there are "tongues" the need for them will disappear, if there is knowledge it will be swallowed up in truth. For our knowledge is always incomplete and our prophecy is always incomplete, and when the Complete comes, that is the end of the Incomplete.

When I was a little child I talked and felt and thought like a little child. Now that I am a man my childish speech and feeling and thought have no further significance for me.

At present we are men looking at puzzling reflections in a mirror. The time will come when we shall see reality whole and face to face! At present all I know is a little fraction of the truth, but the time will come when I shall know it as fully as God now knows me!

In this life we have three great lasting qualities — faith, hope and love. But the greatest of them is love.

$\mathcal{L}$ove $\mathcal{A}$lways $\mathcal{P}$erseveres

[Love] endures, to the last. — *Ronald Knox*

$\mathcal{I}$n 1944, when the United States was in its darkest year of World War II, Ronald Knox published his version of the New Testament in modern language. Knox was one of the first in a long stream of those who followed in his wake, trying desperately to rescue the Scriptures from the Elizabethan English of the King James Version and to allow the Bible to speak for itself in the conversational language of the people.

What Knox could not foresee was the beginning of decades of changes in the American brand of English that would eventually include ghetto street talk, hip talk, the integration of language from foreign cultures such as Mexico and the Far East, and the invention of many new words and drastic changes in many old ones. The clouds of change that were to come with the doctrine of political correctness were not even on the horizon during World

$\mathcal{S}$ure I am of this, that you have only to endure to conquer. You have only to persevere to save yourselves. *Sir Winston Churchill*

War II. However, the Ronald Knox translation, which is not widely read today, was well received by many who were eager for an alternative to the stately King James Version.

With the war years came a fresh focus on the need for family and loved ones. Home was one place where everyone had the potential to create a world that was to our liking, and it was the last place where war-separated families wanted to give despair a foothold. Every soldier idealized his home. And with the end of the war, married love underwent cultural changes. For the first time in history, the decision to stay married became purely voluntary, depending entirely on the depth of commitment there was in a couple's married love.

So when Knox translated Paul's love poem, he must have felt the gravity of this final quality: "Love endures, to the last." Note that he did not say love simply survives, as noble as that may sometimes be. Paul had more in mind than hanging on. Enduring is not a passive act. It calls for courage to conquer whatever may keep us from moving forward. It calls for strength. The word *endurance*, in fact, is Irish in origin and literally means "oak wood"—one of the strongest and most enduring of timbers.

It is fitting that Paul's list of love's qualities concludes with perseverance. For it is only after we have

*G*od Almighty hates a quitter. *Samuel Fessenden*

worked to cultivate patience, kindness, hope, and all the rest, that we truly recognize the wisdom found in love's power to endure. Ask any couple who has been happily married for fifty years if their love life was a cakewalk. You'll be hard pressed to find one. Sure, many seasoned couples focus their memories on the positive side, but every lifelong couple who can look back over the decades together has endured tough times. You can be sure of that. And you can be sure of one other thing: They persevered, not because of legal or social constraints, but because love endures to the last.

Expedients are for the hour, but principles are for the ages. Just because the rains descend, and the winds blow, we cannot afford to build on shifting sands. Henry Ward Beecher

1 Corinthians 13

Translation by Ronald Knox

I can shew you a way which is better than any other.

I may speak with every tongue that men and angels use; yet, if I lack charity, I am no better than echoing bronze, or the clash of cymbals. I may have powers of prophecy, no secret hidden from me, no knowledge too deep for me; I may have utter faith, so that I can move mountains; yet if I lack charity, I count for nothing.

I may give away all that I have, to feed the poor; I may give myself up to be burnt at the stake; if I lack charity, it goes for nothing. Charity is patient, is kind; charity feels no envy; charity is never perverse or proud, never insolent; does not claim its rights, cannot be provoked, does not brood over an injury; takes no pleasure in wrong-doing, but rejoices at the victory of truth; sustains, believes, hopes, endures, to the last.

The time will come when we shall outgrow prophecy, when speaking with tongues will come to an end, when knowledge will be swept away; we shall never have finished with charity. Our knowledge, our prophecy, are only glimpses of the truth; and these glimpses will be swept away when the time of fulfilment comes. (Just so, when I was a child, I talked like a child, I had the intelligence, the thoughts of a child; since I became a man, I have outgrown childish ways.) At present, we are looking at a confused reflection in a mirror; then, we shall see face to face; now I have only glimpses of knowledge; then, I shall recognize God as he has recognized me. Meanwhile, faith, hope and charity persist, all three; but the greatest of them all is charity.

A Poor Reflection

Now all that I know is hazy and blurred, but then I
will see everything clearly. — *Living Bible*

I could never really live the kind of love Paul writes
about."

Leslie blurted out this sentence in frustration just a
few weeks ago as we were reading Paul's love poem
aloud. "Think about it," she continued. "He lists fifteen
characteristics of love, and I don't think I have a lock on
a single one."

"Who does?" I countered. "Do you know any
human being who is always patient, kind, and trusting?
Do you know anyone who is never rude, boastful, or self-
seeking?"

The hard truth is, no mere mortal can ever live by
ideal love alone. We cannot, in this life, be all that love
has the power to make us. Love can become the dominant power in our lives, certainly, but we are not God
and we cannot love as God loves. That's why Paul wraps

*D*uty does not have to be dull. Love can make it beautiful
and fill it with life. *Anonymous*

89

up his poem with a paragraph that pulls no punches. "It's like this," he says. "We can see and understand only a little about God now, as if we were peering at this reflection in a poor mirror . . . now all that I know is hazy and blurred, but then I will see everything clearly."

To fully comprehend Paul's message here, we need to read it as if we were living in Corinth at the time he wrote it. Corinth, you see, was famous for its mirrors. They were made of highly polished metal, and people came from far away to obtain them. However, the metal mirrors didn't come close to reflecting an accurate image. Nothing like the clear images we get from the silver or aluminum mirrors we take for granted in the twentieth century. Corinthian mirrors, at best, reflected a fuzzy figure — the kind you might see on the shiny side of a toaster oven. So when Paul talks about seeing love clearly, not in a "hazy" or "blurred" reflection of a mirror, the people of Corinth immediately understood. And his point is as poignant today as it was in that context: Only God embodies perfect love.

As humans we are severely limited creatures, debilitated by self-seeking. Even the most loving among us cries out for the proverbial scales to be balanced. The most loving still battle a primeval demand for fairness and wants something in return for sacrifice. Love, when we appeal to its power, does help to mute our selfish

Love is giving freely, expecting nothing in return. Law concerns itself with an equitable exchange, this for that. . . .

drives. But somewhere in our soul is a silent scream demanding justice. No matter how loving we become, we want to be loved in return. *It's only fair*, we say with good reason. And it's that same reasoning that turns the power of love into a performance of duty, a duty demanding godly perfection.

True love, however, transforms everything. As Richard McBrain states so elegantly: "Love is . . . at the heart of every other Christian virtue. Thus, for example, justice without love is legalism; faith without love is ideology; hope without love is self-centeredness; forgiveness without love is self-abasement; fortitude without love is recklessness; generosity without love is extravagance; care without love is mere duty; fidelity without love is servitude. Every virtue is an expression of love. No virtue is really a virtue unless it is permeated, or informed, by love."

Paul's profile of perfect love — all fifteen characteristics — was never meant to condemn us for not being perfect lovers. For now, we can be empowered by God's love to momentarily sidestep our self-seeking ways. Love happens alongside our human weakness. That's why perfect love looks so blurry. Someday, Paul says, "I will see everything clearly." And so will all of us who seek a life of love.

. . . Law is made necessary by people; love is made possible by God. *Mary Carson*

1 Corinthians 13

Living Bible

Let me tell you about something else that is better than any of them!

If I had the gift of being able to speak in other languages without learning them, and could speak in every language there is in all of heaven and earth, but didn't love others, I would only be making noise. If I had the gift of prophecy and knew all about what is going to happen in the future, knew everything about *everything*, but didn't love others, what good would it do? Even if I had the gift of faith so that I could speak to a mountain and make it move, I would still be worth nothing at all without love. If I gave everything I have to poor people, and if I were burned alive for preaching the Gospel but didn't love others, it would be of no value whatever.

Love is very patient and kind, never jealous or envious, never boastful or proud, never haughty or selfish or rude. Love does not demand its own way. It is not irritable or touchy. It does not hold grudges and will hardly even notice when others do it wrong. It is never glad about injustice, but rejoices whenever truth wins out. If you love someone you will be loyal to him no matter what the cost. You will always believe in him, always expect the best of him, and always stand your ground in defending him.

All the special gifts and powers from God will someday come to an end, but love goes on forever. Some day prophecy, and speaking in unknown languages, and special knowledge — the gifts will disappear. Now we know so little, even with our special gifts, and the preaching of those most gifted is still so poor. But when we have been made perfect and complete, then the need for these inadequate special gifts will come to an end, and they will disappear.

It's like this: when I was a child I spoke and thought and reasoned as a child does. But when I became a man my thoughts grew far beyond those of my childhood, and now I have put away the childish things. In the same way, we can see and understand only a little about God now, as if we were peering at His reflection in a poor mirror; but someday we are going to see Him in His completeness, face to face. Now all that I know is hazy and blurred, but then I will see everything clearly, just as clearly as God sees into my heart right now.

There are three things that remain — faith, hope, and love — the greatest of these is love.

Afterword

We have a confession. This project of bringing the various translations of Paul's love poem together and writing the meditations to accompany them was done with a hidden agenda. As a couple in our fifteenth year of marriage we long for the kind of love Paul captured in this passage. We long for love in its ideal form.

We want to be patient and kind with one another.

We want to avoid envy, boasting, being proud and rude.

More than anything we want to sidestep our self-seeking ways.

We want to keep anger from hurting our relationship.

We want to bypass records of wrongs and face up to the truths we'd rather ignore.

We want to enjoy the protection, the trust, and the hope that only love can supply.

And, of course, we want our love to persevere.

So we admit it. This little book was written to help us love each other better. We wanted to know how the ideal love of 1 Corinthians 13 — how this perfectly selfless love — could take root in our sometimes selfish lives. We wanted to know how Paul's crystallized qualities of love could sink into our spirit.

Did we accomplish our goal? Have we achieved perfect love? Not exactly. We still admit to impatient moments, angry impulses, jealous surges, and all the rest. We still have needs, drives, and goals that aren't easily harmonized with self-giving love. But we've noticed a difference.

With each reading of this love poem we've come closer to letting it transform us. We've come closer to setting ourselves aside and responding to each other's needs without calculating the costs. The romantic rhapsody lasts for a moment or two before a primeval demand for fairness steals it away. But that's what keeps us coming back to this powerful passage. That's what keeps us reading and rereading love's ideal. Not the promise of perfect love, but the magic of moments where we move toward one another with selfless love — where we are no longer interested in the odds of getting something for ourselves in return for our sacrificial efforts.

With each reading of this love poem, we see more clearly that love is not a duty to perform, but a power that enables. And only the power of love can move us beyond our self-seeking to allow a little of the ideal into the reality of our human impulses.

Love is the *summum bonum* — "the most excellent way." And it is within the grasp of every married couple when we seize the promises of this passage.

Appendix of Bible Translations

Angela McCord (Date Unknown)

This paraphrase of Paul's love poem was written by a student for a classroom exercise. It has not been previously published.

Basic Bible Translation (1950)

Basic English, developed by C. K. Ogden of the Orthological Institute, is a simple form of the English language which uses only 850 words to give the sense of anything which may be said in English. Working with the Orthological Institute in England, a committee under the direction of S. H. Hooks, Professor Emeritus of Old Testament Studies at the University of London, developed this new translation using Basic English. This translation is noted for being straightforward and simple.

Berkeley Version (1945)

This modern translation was edited by Gerrit Verkuyl, Ph.D., D.D., who was on the Presbyterian Board of

Education in Berkeley, California. Greek and Hebrew scholars of various denominations labored on this translation.

Cotton Patch Version of Paul's Epistles by Clarence Jordan (1968)

In this modern-day translation, Paul's letters are taken out of the study and stained-glass sanctuary and placed under God's skies where people toil, laugh, cry, and wonder. The major portion of Clarence Jordan's life was spent on a farm in southwest Georgia where he struggled for a meaningful expression of his discipleship to Jesus Christ. He often worked in fields with dusty rows of cotton, corn, and peanuts. His translation, known as the Cotton Patch Version, is not only a translation into modern American English but also into modern American ideas. In this version, Paul is no longer an artistocratic Pharisee, but a converted Southerner who boldly speaks the mind of Christ on such matters as racism, brotherhood, possessions, church membership and responsibility, the claims of Christ, and personal Christian living. This translation's plain, hard-hitting language is earthy and sweaty, straight from the cotton fields and city streets.

J. B. Phillips (1958)

What started out as one pastor's attempt to make the New Testament understandable to a London youth group eventually turned out to be Phillips' translation. Because the young people "couldn't make head or tail" of the King James Version, J. B. Phillips felt led to translate Paul's letters. And because he happened to send his first attempts at translations to C. S. Lewis, who encouraged him to go on, Phillips' *Letters to Young Churches* was published. C. S. Lewis said of Phillips' first attempt: "It's like seeing an old picture that's been cleaned." Once he completed the Pauline Epistles, Phillips was encouraged by readers from various parts of the world to go on to the Gospels. The entire New Testament was published in 1958.

Wuest's Expanded Translation (1958)

Kenneth S. Wuest was teacher of New Testament Greek at the Moody Bible Institute. This translation was a commentary designed to be used alongside the King James Version. This translation is not easy reading; rather, it demands careful study.

King James Version (1611)

At the same time William Shakespeare was refining his best Elizabethan English in a series of plays that became classics, fifty scholars appointed by King James were at work in Hampton Court translating the Bible into an "authorized" English version. Published in 1611, only three years before Shakespeare died, the King James Version became standard among English-speaking people the world over. Interestingly, the translators almost always translated the Greek word *agape* as *love* throughout the rest of the New

Testament, but in this case they chose the word *charity*. No one knows for sure why, but it may be that charity cannot be reciprocated as love can. And in this poem the kind of love Paul had in mind was ultimate, not based on the person's ability or even willingness to respond in love.

Living Bible (1967)

The title page of the Living Bible reads "paraphrase" on one line and "a thought-by-thought translation" on the next. Kenneth Taylor, a Wheaton, Illinois, businessman, was not trying to have it both ways, but he produced his version with the avowed purpose of making the Bible more understandable to his children. He noted the puzzled expression on the faces of his children — ten in all — when he read to them from the King James Version. When he questioned them regarding their understanding of what he had read, he found they had failed to get the message. He began to reword the Bible in simple, conversational style for his children while riding a commuter train each day from his home in Wheaton to his work in Chicago. He eventually decided to form his own publishing company to promote the paraphrases he was producing. He called his new firm Tyndale House after William Tyndale, the father of the English Bible. Today thousands of readers find they can understand the Living Bible like no other.

The Message (1993)

Eugene Peterson, the author of this paraphrase, is a writer and a professor of spiritual theology at Regent College in Vancouver, British Columbia. His version of the Scriptures uses contemporary English. He observes that the original New Testament was written in the language of the day, the idiom of the playground, and with the sounds and feelings of the marketplace. This version keeps the language of the Bible fresh and understandable.

New American Bible (1970)

In 1944, a committee of prominent Catholic theologians was gathered for the purpose of producing a scholarly translation in harmony with Catholic biblical interpretations. The result was the 1970 publication of the New American Bible. The translation is simple, clear, and straightforward. Its translations are not striking, but neither are they clumsy. They seem to be more conservative in the sense that they tend not to stray from the original.

New International Reader's Version (1995)

This version is based on the popular New International Version. Designed for children, new readers, and people who use English as a second language, this version uses shorter sentences, simple sentence structures, and shorter words to make the Bible even easier to read and understand.

New International Version (1973)

This version attempts to give a more accurate translation of the Bible than the paraphrases and even most modern versions. Many of the scholars who worked for a decade on this translation are known for their evangelical leanings, and the result was an ecumenical effort with dynamic equivalency, rather than rigid translations of exact words. The New International Version holds a distinctive place as being suitable for private reading as well as public worship. It is called an "International" version because the committee producing it consisted of distinguished Bible scholars from around the world. In addition, English is an international language, and the translators sought to use vocabulary common to the major English-speaking nations of the world. Few translations have been as carefully done as this one.

J. Oswald Sanders (Date Unknown)

J. Oswald Sanders studied law at the University of Otago, New Zealand. After serving as superintendent of New Zealand Bible Training Institute in Auckland for a number of years, he became Home Director of the China Inland Mission for Australia and New Zealand. He was then appointed General Director of the Overseas Missionary Fellowship. Following his retirement, he returned to the New Zealand Bible Training Institute.

Ronald Knox (1944)

Ronald Knox was a brilliant student at Oxford who was known for his beautiful prose and detective novels. He began his translation from Greek in 1939 with one governing question: "What would an Englishman have said to express the same idea?" There was distinct clarity in the tone Knox attained in his translation that becomes quite evident in 1 Corinthians 13. For his day, Knox's translation was new and fresh, a welcome contrast to Elizabethan English.

Twentieth Century New Testament (1900)

The story of this translation begins in 1861 when a letter from a Congregational minister in England was sent to a magazine editor, expressing his desire to have a translation that would make the meaning of the Bible plain to youth and uneducated people. With this letter serving as a catalyst, a group of twenty like-minded translators began their work. Half of the translators were ministers and the rest included housewives, businessmen, and schoolteachers. In the original preface to this translation, Edward Deacon Girdlestone gave the purpose of their work: "To enable Englishmen to read the most important part of their Bible in that form of their own language which they themselves use." He expressed the fear that the retention of the Scriptures in a form of English no longer in common use "is liable to give the impression that the contents of the Bible have little to do with the life of today."

William Barclay (1954)

This popular Scottish teacher and preacher had a passion for helping the informed layperson understand Scripture in its cultural context and relate it to today's world. To that end he wrote a popular Bible commentary, in which he included his own Bible translation. His translation of the Bible is not available as a separate book but is incorporated into his commentary, which has been used profitably for half a century by thousands of serious Bible students around the world. This portion from 1 Corinthians is excerpted from Barclay's commentary titled *The Letters to the Corinthians*.

Becoming Soul Mates

52 Meditations to Bring Joy
to Your Marriage

*B*ecoming Soul Mates gives you a
road map for cultivating rich
spiritual intimacy in your relationship.   Fifty-two practical weekly
devotions help you and your partner
dig deep for a strong spiritual foun-
dation in the early years of marriage.

In each session you will find:

- An insightful devotion that
  focuses on marriage-related
  topics
- A key passage of Scripture
- Questions that will spark discussions on crucial
  issues
- Insights from real-life soul mates like Pat and
  Shirley Boone, Bill and Vonette Bright, and
  more
- Questions that will help you and your partner
  better understand each other's unique needs
  and remember them in prayer during the week.

Start building on the closeness you've got today—
and reap the rewards of a deep, more satisfying relationship in the years ahead.

Hardcover 0-310-20014-8

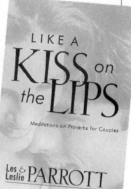

We want to hear from you. Please send your comments about this book to us in care of zreview@zondervan.com. Thank you.

GRAND RAPIDS, MICHIGAN 49530 USA

WWW.ZONDERVAN.COM